21st
Century
Skills Library

COOL CAREERS

VIDEO GAME DESIGNER

Kevin Cunningham

Cherry Lake Publishing
Ann Arbor, Michigan

Published in the United States of America by Cherry Lake Publishing
Ann Arbor, Michigan
www.cherrylakepublishing.com

Content Adviser: Zhenelle Falk, Video Game Producer, 1st Playable Productions, LLC

Photo Credits: Cover and page 1, ©AP Photo/Ric Francis; page 4, ©AP Photo/Paul
Sakuma; page 6, ©Sinibomb Images/Alamy; page 7, ©ArcadeImages/Alamy; page 10,
©Purestock/Alamy; page 13, ©Frances Roberts/Alamy; pages 14 and 22, ©iStockphoto.
com/track5; page 15, ©iStockphoto.com/Claudiad; page 17, ©Picture Contact/Alamy;
page 18, ©iStockphoto.com/stray_cat; page 21, ©forestpath, used under license from
Shutterstock, Inc.; page 25, ©vario images GmbH & Co.KG/Alamy; page 26, ©David L.
Moore-Lifestyle/Alamy

Library of Congress Cataloging-in-Publication Data
Cunningham, Kevin, 1966–
Video game designer / by Kevin Cunningham.
   p. cm.—(Cool careers)
ISBN-13: 978-1-60279-305-7
ISBN-10: 1-60279-305-0
1. Video games—Design—Vocational guidance—Juvenile literature.
2. Video games industry—Vocational guidance—Juvenile literature. I. Title.
II. Series.
GV1469.3.C86 2009
794.8'1536—dc22   2008006519

*Cherry Lake Publishing would like to acknowledge the work of
The Partnership for 21st Century Skills.
Please visit www.21stcenturyskills.org for more information.*

TABLE OF CONTENTS

CHAPTER ONE

THE EVOLUTION OF VIDEO GAMES

Shigeru Miyamoto of Nintendo is one of the world's top video game designers.

"Stephen, we have an issue!" exclaimed a worried co-worker. "For some reason, the game crashes at the end of the Werewolf Bay cut scenes. Also, there's a collision bug that sends the main character falling through the floor. We need to figure out why these glitches are happening!"

"Don't worry. I'll get the programmers to work on the collision bug and the crash bug," Stephen said calmly. Stephen is a video game designer who loves his job. He enjoys coming up with creative ideas for cool video games. Being a video game designer means solving problems. It also means long hours and dealing with tough deadlines. But Stephen knows that his job is unique and exciting. His work helps bring entertainment to millions of people worldwide.

Video games date as far back as the 1960s. In 1968, engineer Ralph H. Baer designed a video game console that could play simple games on a television. Baer's Magnavox Odyssey, also known as the Brown Box, was released in 1972. It was a huge success.

Bushnell started the Atari Corporation in the 1970s. The company released the Atari 2600 and sold 20 million units.

Not long after Baer's revolutionary invention, a video game fan named Nolan Bushnell had an innovation of his own. Adopting Baer's table tennis game on the Odyssey system, Bushnell created a video ping-pong game called

Donkey Kong was a popular arcade game in the 1980s. The graphics are very simple compared to today's games.

Pong for arcades. Soon Bushnell created a game console for *Pong* that hooked up to the TV set in the home. *Pong* is considered the first home video game hit.

Each new generation of video games appeared with better sound and graphics. Improvements in artificial intelligence encouraged more people to play. Sports games, such as

Madden NFL, put players in the middle of National Football League action. Strategy-based games, such as *Sim City* and *Civilization*, encouraged gamers to build their own cities and societies. Role-playing video games, such as the *Final Fantasy* series, came with cutting-edge graphics and game play. As games became more complex, designers needed teams of programmers, artists, and others to help create better games. Designers provided ideas and served as team leaders.

The mid-1990s saw video games grow into a vital part of the entertainment industry. The rise of the Internet helped fuel the rise of another kind of game—massively multiplayer online role-playing games (MMORPG). Games such as *Everquest*, and later *World of Warcraft*, allow millions of players to log into an online fantasy world and interact with one another.

In 2007, the video game industry generated a record $18.85 billion in sales. Video game production companies are growing by leaps and bounds. The industry needs talented video game designers like never before. Let's look at how a video game designer uses his or her skills and talents to create great video games.

CHAPTER TWO

ON THE JOB

Most video game designers work in a casual environment.

Video game designers are the quarterbacks of the video game design team. A designer leads a group of talented people with many different skills. The video game development team consists of computer programmers, artists, animators, writers, sound designers, composers, and many others. The design team collaborates to create games for consoles, computers, and online play.

When a design team plans on making a new video game, there is a process to follow. A new game starts with the lead designer. The designer gathers a team of people together to brainstorm video game ideas. Lead designers may get ideas for games from the production company they work for or from fans and gamers. The team asks various questions such as: What kind of a game do we want to create? Where does it take place? Who are the main characters? How will the game compare to other games on the market? The lead designer and design team come up with the answers to these questions. These answers will help determine what is to be done next.

After the brainstorming meeting, the team sketches out the plot of the game's story. The team comes up with the player's goals. They also decide what challenges

Learning & Innovation Skills

Early in the process, the artistic level designer works with basic visual guides called proxies to lay out areas of the game environment. The details we see—whether stone castles, towering redwoods, or the inside of a submarine—are dropped in later on after being created by the artists and animators.

Artistic level designers must be able to develop new ideas and communicate them to others. Their vision is what others will use to bring a video game to life.

the main character must overcome. The team also thinks about where the game's story will take place. Exactly how the game will be played must also be determined. These ideas will all go into a **game design document** (GDD). The GDD acts as the guide for creating the game. The design team will use the GDD to stay on schedule throughout the project. The lead designer is responsible for keeping the GDD up-to-date with changes and new ideas.

Video game designers learn how to do their jobs through experience. By working on design teams, they have learned how to get a game from the idea stage into the hands of eager gamers.

*Video game designers work out game details that
most ordinary players may not notice.*

Video game designers also play a lot vof video games. By playing games created by others, the designer learns what the competition is doing. An experienced video game designer can explain what is good or bad about a game in great detail. That's because designers don't just play video games. They study them, too.

It is important for the lead designer to work well with others on the team.

Ideas, creativity, and leadership are essential to being a successful video game designer. But a lead designer cannot build a game on his or her own. A lead designer depends on certain people to keep a project moving forward. One of the lead designer's most trusted partners is the video game producer. The producer oversees the day-to-day

*Game producers must have good communication skills
and be able to keep track of a lot of information.*

operation of a project. Producers recruit people to work

on a new game. They also create the project schedule

and they are in charge of the budget. As a project moves

forward, producers meet with artists, programmers,

and others on the development team. A producer's

main job is to make sure that all the departments are working together smoothly.

The video game designer also depends on level designers. Level designers are in charge of creating the details for each level in the new game. Level designers will split up responsibilities. There is a level designer in charge of the artistic elements of the game. Another level designer is in charge of making sure the game plays the right way. The lead designer works with the level designers to set goals. The lead designer also makes sure that each level fits with the game's story.

*Creating a video game character takes patience
and close attention to detail.*

A job as a lead designer comes with a lot of
responsibility, guaranteeing a busy workday. There are
endless decisions to be made. It's not a job that just anyone
can handle. To rise to the top of the profession takes
dedication, talent, and a lot of training.

CHAPTER THREE

EDUCATION AND TRAINING

Most video game designers started playing video games when they were kids.

Are you creative and artistic? Do you love playing video games? Think you might want to become a video game designer? You can start training for a career in video game design now. There are plenty of ways you can build up your skills for the future.

First, you should be playing video games! But don't just play the games. Think about them, too. While playing, pause the game and think creatively about what's going on. Could different music make a scene better? How would you make that monster in front of you scarier? Is the level you're playing too easy, too fast, too slow? Is the game boring? What works? What doesn't work? Video game designers think about these kinds of questions every day. Thinking critically about games helps designers come up with ways to create better games.

In high school, classes in computer programming languages are a good place to start. It also helps to study the sciences. Physics helps you understand large systems. All of these skills are handy later on when you are designing your own video games.

Artistic ability helps, too. Art classes provide you with a background in painting and drawing. Taking these classes can help you develop solid visual skills. Audio and music are video game elements as well. Pick up an instrument and learn how to play. Take a music class, or join the school band. Understanding how sound and music work helps spark ideas.

Your education doesn't stop in high school. Today's video game designers usually have a college degree. Many universities offer a four-year degree in video game design. For those interested in specialized training, technical schools such as Digitech, Full Sail, or DeVry Institute prepare students to work in the industry. Your college work will include a lot of computer science. Classes in graphics, artificial intelligence, and software engineering help future designers deal with technical issues.

Playing an instrument may improve memory and learning ability in children. These skills are useful as a game designer.

Summer break allows students to get an edge. Game companies offer summer internships. These are paid or unpaid positions that let students get on-the-job training. Interns have a chance to demonstrate their growing skills and talents. An intern who is able to impress the company's supervisors may be offered a job after graduation.

*Being comfortable with computers and technology
is a must for game designers.*

21st CENTURY SKILLS LIBRARY

Many people start their designer careers as game testers. This position is known as quality assurance (QA). Game testers play early versions of a game in order to find mistakes, or "bugs." QA certifies games that are considered ready to be released. Not everyone starts in QA. Someone's first job may be as a sound technician, programmer, or artist. From these positions, an employee may rise to higher positions such as lead designer or producer.

A would-be designer needs determination to get his or her ideas heard. Those ideas must fit in with what the team can create on time. Designers must also consider the budget and the

Do you think a job as a game tester sounds like fun? It can be if you enjoy playing the same level of a game over and over again. Why do testers have to do this? That is the only way to find all of the bugs in the game. A good game tester understands the importance of finding bugs. Successful QA team members are excellent at paying attention to details. They try to think of every possible way of playing through a level. Game testers are crucial members of the teams that create new video games.

Learning & Innovation Skills

Some games allow anyone to take a crack at design. For example, certain versions of the skateboarding game *Tony Hawk's Proving Ground* have tools that allow players to customize a skater and edit the game's video.

If a game you own comes with such tools, check them out. Be inventive! Tinker with aspects of the game. Make decisions and choices about how you want your version to look. Learn how a small change leads to creating something new. See how your new version plays. Go online to check out work done by others, and compare your version to theirs.

People interested in a career in video game design sometimes create Web sites with examples of how they've edited existing games. These edits are referred to as "mods," short for modifications. This can be an excellent tool for showing a production company what you can do.

people available to work on the project. A designer needs to have the experience to know what it takes to finish a project. That's why it's important that your education and training give you an idea of what others can (and cannot) do. The ability to carry a project from the idea stage to the final product is what separates the best game designers from the rest.

CHAPTER FOUR

THE NEXT LEVEL

At conventions, designers and game lovers get a chance to check out the latest releases.

Today's video game companies are looking for ideas that can cross over into media beyond the gaming world. Doing this helps companies create more products and make more money.

The Nintendo Wii uses a special controller that senses movement.

Games with a possible tie-in to movies are desirable. The fighting game *Mortal Kombat* was turned into a film in 1995. In the early 2000s, Hollywood turned the video game adventure classic *Tomb Raider* into a popular film.

Rumor has it that a film version of the science fiction game *Halo* may be out in early 2009. These kinds of crossovers can only strengthen the video game industry.

Video games may be completely different 10 or 20 years from now. Designers, companies, and gamers alike look to technology and how it will change things. Computers will become more powerful. Games will feature new images, new kinds of sounds, and better game-play. Gamers may begin to have more freedom to alter game elements. The latest advances already point to a day when games equipped with sensors react to our body movements. The Nintendo Wii is a perfect example. It's possible that game systems worn on our heads will soon project images directly onto the retinas behind our eyes. All of these advances

Game designers are sometimes called the rock stars of the industry. Their creativity, innovation, and leadership are what drive the industry to new heights. But the job doesn't guarantee fame. It's unusual when the public learns a video game designer's name. Instead, we usually associate a game with the company that puts it out. Far more people have heard of Relic Entertainment than of John Carmack or Jason Jones. Some believe that game creation will one day be recognized as an art form. If this turns out to be true, video game designers may become as famous as movie directors and novelists.

will present designers with an opportunity to take games in new directions.

The video game industry is here to stay. The top four games in 2007—*Halo 3*, *Wii Play*, *Call of Duty 4*, and *Guitar Hero III*—together sold more than 14.7 million copies. And research shows that gamers continue to play as adults, too. As today's players grow up, and new fans join in every year, video games will provide exciting careers for the next wave of designers.

Some Famous Video Game Designers

Nolan Bushnell (1943–) founded Atari in 1972. Atari's game *Pong*, played through a console hooked to a TV set, became the first popular home video game. He went on to develop games such as *PacMan* and *Pitfall*, which became timeless classics. Bushnell was given the Lifetime Achievement Award from the Video Game Hall of Fame in 2005.

John Carmack (1970–) is the brilliant computer programmer who masterminded the first three-dimensional (3-D) game in the 1990s with *Castle Wolfenstein*. His company, id Software, later released the classic role-playing video games *Doom* and *Quake*.

Jason Jones (?–) co-founded Bungie Studios production company while still in college. He led the teams behind the popular Xbox games *Halo* and *Halo 2*. He is one of the hottest new video game designers today.

Sid Meier (1954–) started MicroProse in 1982 and released the strategy-based game *Civilization* in 1991. As the head of Firaxis Games, Meier continues to produce new versions of the highly popular *Civilization* series.

Shigeru Miyamoto (1952–) is Nintendo's greatest visionary and is considered one of the top innovators in the industry's history. He began his career as an artist. His classic video games, such as *Donkey Kong* and *Super Mario Bros.*, made Nintendo into a video-gaming icon.

Will Wright (1960–) co-founded Maxis, Inc., in 1987 in Orinda, California. His *The Sims*, released in 2000 by Electronic Arts, is currently the best-selling computer game ever.

Glossary

arcades (ar-KAYDZ) rooms or businesses where people pay to play games

artificial intelligence (ar-ti-FISH-uhl in-TEL-uh-juhnss) the capability of a machine to control everything not under the control of the player

budget (BUHJ-it) a plan mapping out how money will be spent on a project

franchise (FRAN-chize) a group of related games, or one game and its sequels

game design document (GAME di-ZINE DOK-yuh-muhnt) a written plan that lays out a game's characters, obstacles, goals, and other details

generation (jen-uh-RAY-shuhn) a type of object developed from an earlier type

internships (IN-turn-ships) short-term jobs with a company that are set aside for students, who learn new skills on the job

media (MEE-dee-uh) a means of communication to a large number of people

proxies (PRAK-zees) simple visual guides (usually without details) placed into a game and filled in later

technical schools (TEK-nuh-kuhl SKOOLZ) special kinds of colleges that train students for jobs in certain industries

FOR MORE INFORMATION

Books

Burns, Jan. *Shigeru Miyamoto.* San Diego: KidHaven Press, 2006.

Ferguson Careers in Focus. *Computer and Video Game Design.* New York: Facts on File, 2005.

Gerardi, David, and Peter Suciu. *Careers in the Computer Game Industry.* New York: Rosen Publishing Group, 2005.

Web Sites

A Digital Dreamer
www.adigitaldreamer.com/articles/becomeavideogamedesigner.htm
Read more about how to become a video game
designer and what it takes to be successful

DigiPen Institute of Technology
www.digipen.edu/main/Main_Page
Browse through the DigiPen Institute's site to find out more
about its video game design program

INDEX

ABOUT THE AUTHOR

Kevin Cunningham is the author of 30 books, including a series on diseases in history and a number of books in Cherry Lake's Global Products series. He lives near Chicago, Illinois.